EARS

HUMAN BODY

Robert James

The Rourke Press, Inc.
Vero Beach, Florida 32964

PHOTO CREDITS
All photos © Kyle Carter except title page and page 21 © Frank
Balthis and page 17 © Busch Entertainment Corporation. All rights
reserved.

Library of Congress Cataloging-in-Publication Data

James, Robert, 1942-
    Ears / by Robert James.
        p. cm. — (Human body)
    Includes index.
    Summary: Describes the anatomy of the human ear and
includes information on ear problems, care of the ear, and the ears
of some animals.
    ISBN 1-57103-102-2
    1. Ear—Anatomy—Juvenile literature.   [1. Ear.]
I. Title II. Series: James, Robert, 1942-   Human body
QM507.J36   1995
611.85—dc20   95–19000
                                                              CIP
                                                              AC

Printed in the USA

TABLE OF CONTENTS

THE EAR

Your ears are partners with your brain. Together, they allow you to hear.

These hearing partners, the ears and brain, help make lives easier and more enjoyable. They bring us the sounds of words, music, rain, and wind. They also bring us the sounds that warn us of danger, such as sirens and screams.

Like your eyes, your ears help you know what is going on around you.

Ears can help us recognize danger, like a rattlesnake, and avoid it!

THE OUTER EAR

The ear that you see is only part of the package. You see the outer ear, a flap of skin that covers a frame of **cartilage** (KART el idj). Cartilage is a tough, but very **flexible** (FLEHX uh bul) material. Because there are no bones in the outer ear, we can bend it easily without breaking it.

You also can see an earlobe at the base of the ear flap. Just above the earlobe is the opening to your inner ear. That opening is the beginning of a passageway called the ear canal.

The outer ear flap covers a frame of cartilage

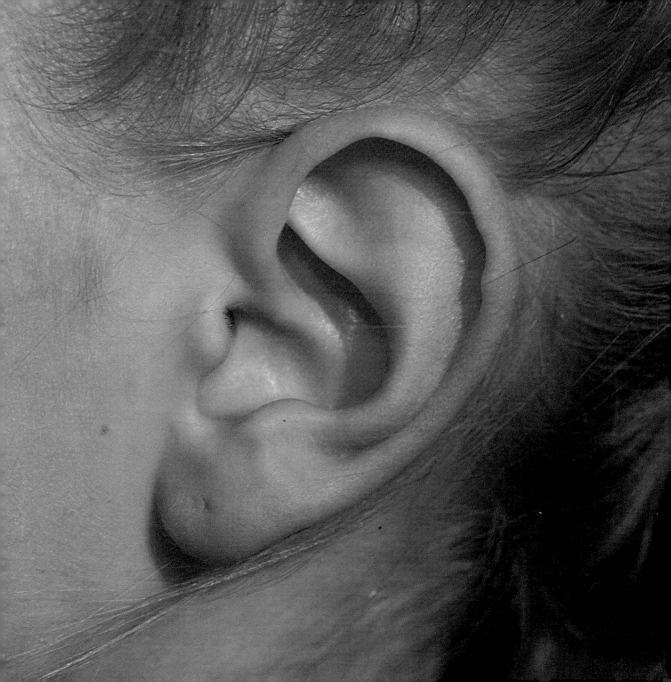

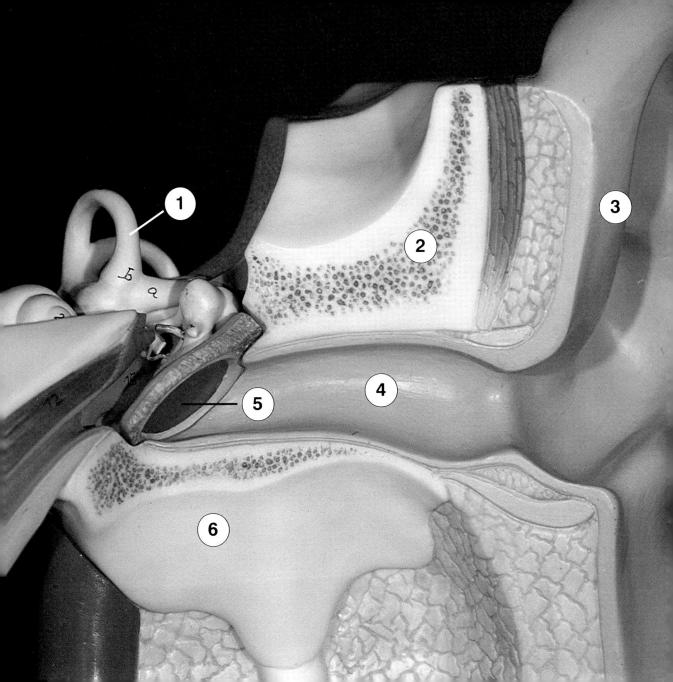

INSIDE THE EAR

The ear canal leads to the **eardrum** (EAR drum), the middle ear, and the inner ear. The drum and other parts of the ear work together. Along with the brain, they make it possible for you to hear.

Three little bones in each ear play an important part in hearing. One of those bones, the stirrup, is the smallest bone in the body. It is smaller than an apple seed!

1. Inner ear balance tubes
2. Bone
3. Outer ear
4. Outer ear canal
5. Eardrum
6. Bone

SOUNDS

A sound is something we hear. A sound is also a moving wave of air. When we speak, we send out a **vibration** (vi BRAY shun), an air wave. We can't see air waves, but our ears can "capture" them—or some of them.

Human ears are not sensitive to every sound. Dogs, for example, can hear certain sounds that are beyond the ability of human hearing.

This German Shepard's ears can hear sounds that his master's ears cannot

The great, fanlike ears of an African elephant shed heat, direct sounds, and send messages in body language to other elephants

Human ears can pick up gentle sounds like humming and whispering

THE EAR AND BRAIN

Your ears are receivers. They receive messages from the air waves that enter them.

Along with your eardrums and other inner ear structures are tiny **nerves** (NERVZ). The nerves send messages to the brain.

The brain instantly computes the information from the nerve messages. We receive that information as sounds, such as laughter, yelling, shouting, hissing, and talking.

Airwaves travel from a radio to your ears and on to your brain

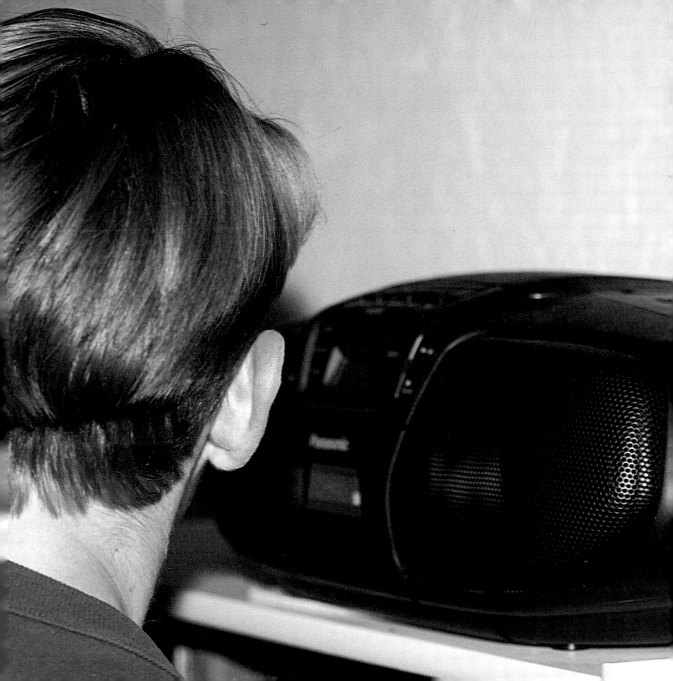

EARS AND BALANCE

The inner ear holds liquid in balance tubes. When the inner ear and balance tubes work properly, you feel "normal."

Sudden up and down movements on roller coasters cause a shift of liquid in balance tubes. That briefly creates a falling or "elevator" sensation.

The whirling of merry-go-rounds also affects balance tubes. When the motion first stops, the balance tubes tell the brain you are still moving. Your eyes say "no movement." Your confused brain makes you feel dizzy.

Roller coasters, such as the Scorpion at Busch Gardens, Tampa Bay, shown here, and elevators cause movements of liquid in the balance tubes of the inner ear

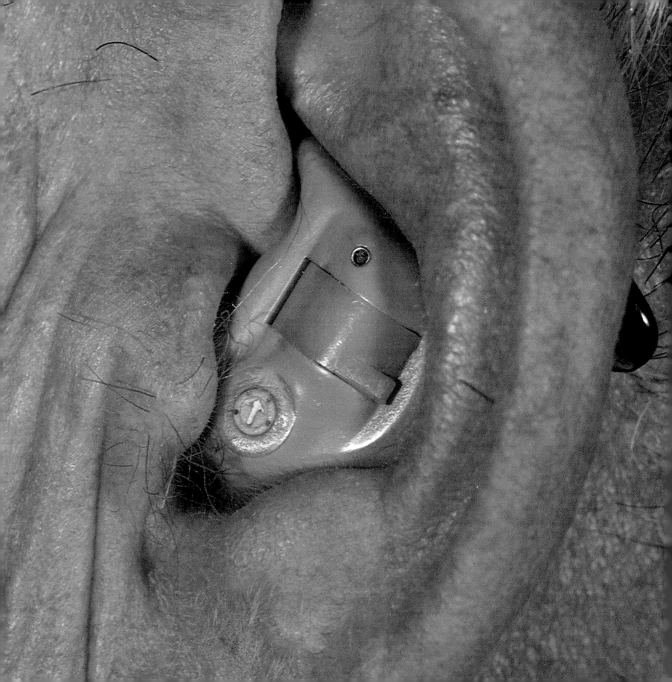

EAR PROBLEMS

Many things can cause some loss of hearing, or deafness. Disease, head injuries, burns, and loud noises can damage or destroy hearing.

Scuba divers sometimes damage their ears because of sudden changes in the water pressure against their eardrums.

Doctors can sometimes repair damage to the middle ear and improve someone's hearing. Damage to the inner ear cannot be repaired.

A hearing aid helps many people who have some loss of hearing

EAR CARE

Treating your ears with care will help protect them. Start by keeping sharp objects away from your ears. You could break an eardrum with a sharp object.

If ear wax becomes a problem, have a doctor remove it. Ear wax traps dust and dirt; it's good for your ears, but it can build up now and then.

Avoid being around loud noises for long periods of time. Loud noises can cause hearing loss.

Heavy equipment operators use ear protectors to muffle engine noise

ANIMAL EARS

The largest outer ears in the animal kingdom belong to the elephant. The elephant's giant ear flaps serve several purposes. Their wide surface helps the elephant shed extra body heat. The way an elephant holds its ears can help it tell another elephant whether it is angry, nervous, or relaxed.

Dogs and owls have extremely fine hearing. The owl's long outer "ears," however, are just feathers, not ears.

Glossary

cartilage (KART el idj) — strong, flexible body tissue found in the outer ear and nose

eardrum (EAR drum) — in the inner ear, a small, thin, round piece of skin that is sensitive to sound waves

flexible (FLEHX uh bul) — able to bend easily and often

nerves (NERVZ) — the sensitive "feelers" in flesh that send messages to the brain

vibration (vi BRAY shun) — movement that sends sounds to the ear

INDEX